The Hide of My Tongue

Ax̱ L'óot' Doogú

poems by

Vivian Faith Prescott

Plain View Press
http://plainviewpress.net

3800 N. Lamar, Suite 730-260
Austin, TX 78756

ISBN: 978-1-935514-87-9
Library of Congress Control Number: 2011945373

Front Cover art: Tlingit Totem pole from Klawock, Alaska,
        Courtesy of Tommy Joseph, *Naal xák'w*
Back Cover: Saanaheit House Post from Old Kasaan. Replica was carved
        by Tommy Joseph. Sitka National Historic Park, Sitka, Alaska.
Photo by Aanguk, Howie Martindale, Wooshkeetaan, Shark House.
Cover design by Pam Knight

To

Our elders and Lingít language teachers
and all the learners who are working to revitalize
and save our precious languages

and
to my daughter, Yéilk'—Cute Little Raven—
who inspires others to learn.

Acknowledgments

Grateful acknowledgment is made to the following publications in which these poems or earlier versions appeared.

"Time of Silence," *River Poets Journal*; "Annie" and "Telling Bones," *Explorations* (2000, 2001); "I know there is a name for you," *Permafrost* (2007); "Extinction" and "Lingít Oratory," *Ice Box* (2008); "Struggling with My Language," "Cephalic Index," and "Role Model," *Tidal Echoes* (2007, 2009); "The Last Word" won honorable mention in the 2009 Harold McCracken Poetry Contest at the University of Alaska Fairbanks and appeared in *Tidal Echoes* (2010); "Disturbing the Tourists at Glacier Bay National Park," *Arcadia* (2010); "*Tundatáan yák'w*," *Lishanu*; "Traditions," *Alaska Women Speak* (2010); "Saliva," "Sociology 101," "Lingua Nullius," *Milk Sugar*; "Wash Day" and "Struggling with My Language," *Memory*; "The-Place-for-Hunting-Snowy-Owls," and "Know My Skin," *EarthSpeak Magazine*; "English Lessons," and "Indian Gerber," *Solo Novo: Wall Scrawls*; "Your Emergence" and "Creating the Sacred," *Ithaca Lit*; "Halleluiah Fire at the Wrangell Institute," "Language Development," "Talk-Like-an-American" and "Tight Tongues and Open Spaces," *Yellow Medicine Review*.

I am indebted to Daphne (Duffy) Wright, K̲'ashkegé, of Hoonah, Alaska, for the opportunity to learn the Lingít language at Hoonah City Schools and for opening the doors for my whole family to be able to learn. After three generations, my family is the first to be able to speak to one another in the Lingít language. I am also grateful to Carol Williams, *Yeidukdudei, X̲eindusxee,* of Hoonah, Alaska, for her friendship and mentoring. As well, I appreciate Sealaska Heritage Institute for providing the opportunity for my family and me to participate in the Lingít language immersion camps. I also owe a debt of gratitude to Richard and Nora Dauenhauer and Lance Twitchell for their language resources. And I am especially thankful to Lance Twitchell, X̲'unei, Du Aaní Kawdinóok, K̲'eijáakw, M.F.A., Assistant Professor of Native Languages at the University of Alaska Southeast, Juneau for his expertise concerning the Tlingit language portions of this manuscript. Lance Twitchell also created the study guide which is included at the end of this collection.

Contents

Foreword by Vivian K. Mork

Tsu héidi shuga̱xtootáan yá yaakoosgé dakeit haa jeex' a ná̱k has kawdik'éet'.
— Kichnáalx̱

We will open again this container of wisdom left in our care.
—George Davis, Kichnáalx̱

The pride in learning your native language is a big change from past generations. We've come a long way from the boarding school generation who was forbidden to speak its languages. When you look through old government documents, you find references that the government knew that in order to get rid of the "Nativeness" in Native peoples, they had to remove children from their homes, their culture, their influences, and take away their customs and language. Because language and culture are intertwined, the government schools had to take it away to assimilate them—it was almost successful.

But it wasn't just the boarding school experiences that created the loss of our language; it began with epidemics such as smallpox and tuberculosis. These diseases wiped out entire villages, including their traditional knowledge and language.

Also, there were entire generations of people who decided that the language was dead and let it go. This came after the push to assimilate Natives into mainstream American society. There were reasons why people went to the schools and reasons why people sent their family members away to get educated. Native peoples knew change was coming. They needed to be ready, and one way was to educate leaders within the Western system. But it didn't have to be done in such a traumatic way.

Although the process of relearning the language is difficult, through learning, both young and older students have been changed. There are people who have decided to dedicate their lives to learning the Lingít language and have devoted themselves to making sure it will never die. It's changed how we language-learners relate with one another; knowing we are going to interact with each other for the rest of our lives, we treat each other with respect.

Despite the lack of natural settings, teaching in the school system is important. When children start to learn the language, they realize where their pride can come from. We tell them that they have been here since time immemorial and that this land is theirs—they belong to it. When they really know who they are in the language, no one can take that away from them. This is amazing to hold on to; it makes their spirits stronger. After all, the Lingít language is such an elaborate language. It needs to be lived. It is a living language.

Vivian K. Mork
Yéilk' (Cute Little Raven), M.A.
CCS, Indigenous Knowledge Systems
Lingít language and cultural specialist.

Of the eight hundred Native American languages, more than five hundred are in danger of extinction. In southeast Alaska and western Canada, the Lingít language is one of them. There are less than three hundred fluent Tlingit speakers left in the world.

Right from the very beginning I identified with each poem, those of the younger years with the most impact. No one understood me then or in school. Many times I was given the taste of soap to wash the Tlingit out of my mind and speech. I managed to run away from that dismal [orphanage] when I was about three or four years old. I wanted my father again to protect me. My mother died when I was very young. But I was caught and dragged back. I fought mightily, but the boy who caught me was bigger and much stronger than I was. I, too, was silent for much of that time and still am today.

— Deisheetaan, Tlingit elder and WWII veteran Roy Bailey, *Kaaxoo.átch, Saant.éex*, Sitka, Alaska (1926-2011).

Tlingit Introduction According to Protocol

Yéilk' Tláa yoo x̱at duwasáakw ku.aa Dleit K̲áa X̱'éináx̱ Vivian Faith Prescott. Yéil naa k̲a T'ak̲déintaanx̱ x̱at sitee. Tax̱' Hít yoo duwasáakw haa naa kahídi. Sáami k̲a Suomalaiset k̲a Irish k̲a Norwegian k̲a English k̲a German yádi áyá x̱at. Howie Martindale yoo duwasáakw ax̱ x̱úx̱. Mitchell Prescott áwé ax̱ éesh sáayi, k̲a Lorna Woods áwé ax̱ tláa. Ax̱ léelk'w has áwé Binkley k̲a Amundsen. K̲aachx̱ana.áak'wx' áwé x̱at k̲oowdzitee, k̲a Sheet'káx' yei x̱at yatee yeedát. Gunalchéesh.

My Tlingit name is Mother-of-Cute-Little Raven and my English name is Vivian Faith Prescott. I'm adopted *T'ak̲deintaan*. My family and I belong to the *T'ak̲deintaan* clan, and our clan house is called the Snail House. I'm a child of the Sáami, Suomalainen, Irish, Norwegian, English, and German peoples. My husband's name is Howie Martindale. My father's name is Mitchell Prescott, and my mother's is Lorna Woods. My grandparents are the Binkleys and the Amundsens. I was born in Wrangell, Alaska, and now reside in Sitka, Alaska. Thank you.

I.

They must adjust to their environment and conform to our civilization …
They cannot escape it, and must either conform to it or be crushed by it.

> — Thomas J. Morgan, commissioner, "Report of the
> Commissioner of Indian Affairs," 1889

Yee yoo x̲'atángi áwé haa sinéix̲ a yáx̲ yatee x̲'áal' a káx' haa s'éil' x̲'éiyi.
> –Keet Yaanaayí

Your words are healing like the skunk cabbage applied to our open
wounds.

> —Paraphrased from a speech by Willie Marks, *Keet Yaanaayí*
> with translation help by Ethel Makinen, *Daasdiyáa*, and Irene
> Paul, *Yaax̲l.aat*

Journal of Loss

I.

It's her first day of school.
She says to the teacher,
Tlél a̠x daa yaa ̠kushusgé, Tlél a̠x daa yaa ̠kushusgé
        I do not understand, I do not understand
and she keeps repeating the Lingít words
until they slap her hand with a ruler.

She looks down at the sting,
repeats in her language, *I do not understand,*
and she's led away to the closet,
already prepared with a little bed
and thin blanket.

She's shut in tight, door locked;
in the dark she thinks about
darkness,
wonders what bad thing
they thought she had spoken.
Sixty years later, she says
I thought the world had come to an end.
It did,
I think to myself,
It did.

II.

They say I'm shy because I don't say anything,
don't raise my hand,
don't interrupt, but I was told my words
hold power, so if I start talking
I might not stop, because the things I have to say
are not a one-word answer. Words, if spoken,
might shape themselves into killer whales

made of yellow cedar, and mosquitoes
rising from the ashes—
Sometimes, it's good to be quiet.

III.

They give me a Native corporation check
every October, sometimes in April or July—
enough to buy groceries for the month.
First, they said to call them Indian Checks,
then it was Native Money,
now it's a Dividend, because I'm a Shareholder,
a shareholder of what...words?
I think there's a change in dialect
going on—It's still my Grocery Money.

IV.

My daughter goes off to college,
learns to speak the Tlingit language,
learns there are books and recordings
of elder's speeches and words
she thought long gone. She learns so well
now she teaches the elders who don't know
there's a way to write and read their own language.
She teaches them where to put the apostrophes,
underlines, and tone marks. But they tell her
she speaks "university Lingít."

V.

We speak encouragement:
i gu.aa yáx̱ x'wán —have strength, have courage
when someone is unable to speak
because of overwhelming emotion,
and it's proper to go and stand beside them.
The elder, who taught my daughter
at the university, rises to stand beside her.
My daughter is crying, though not because
she should not speak
Lingít here, nor because she cannot speak
or understand her own language,
she is crying, because today
is the day she *can* speak, *Lingít X̱'éináx̱*.
     It's a good day to speak.

Vivian Faith Prescott

Invitation to Feast—_K_oo.éex'

Today, I'm your host as you enter the world
inside my mouth, where salmon leap
to the back of my throat,

and my uvular chatters like a blue jay
among alder. Here, wolves ramble
up hills, and coho, black bear, and eagle play

near the house posts of my teeth. I'll feed you
words like seal oil dripping on herring eggs;
dance a blanket of air wrapped around us,

thudding on the hide of my tongue.
We'll sing a peculiar clatter, ruffling black
feathers beneath blankets, bending arms,

flapping wings, while tipping our heads
back to caw. We'll hold council here,
speaking with unpressed lips, rocking sounds,

rounding letters in mid word; balance
our voices, listening for the difference
in pitch between tree root and salmon.

And when you're ready to leave my house,
please, if your world becomes unpalatable,
you may host a feast and enter dancing

inside your mouth, thumping on nippled tongue,
talking stick in hand, offering the gift
of cheeks full of words.

Absence

rocking child in the airport
six years old
going "out" to boarding school
rocking child
rocking child
I want to comfort you
but I'm too afraid
I can still hear my own
grandmother crying
propellers whirring

there's silence in the village
all the children are gone

and the little ones
are rocking themselves in the airport
rocking
       rocking
              rocking

Vivian Faith Prescott

Time of Silence

Quiet.
The village is quiet.

At home, she puts the moose meat in the pot,
her grandson's favorite meal.
She eats alone. Later, he writes her a letter

in English and she smiles—he's learning.
At night she walks down the boardwalk
to the store and pauses, snow

swirls around her feet. Like the other
grandmothers and grandfathers,
she's become accustomed to this quiet,
the dim lights in their windows.

Even the lights in the sky no longer dance.
Fading light, fading
noise

fading again
to quiet.

With crying children, the plane is gone,
its drone hollowed. Weeping parents
and grandparents remain like dying salmon
on riverbanks.

Halleluiah Fire at the Wrangell Institute

Grandmother sewed the best parka
for grandson's stay at the boarding school;

rick-rack borders, spotted seal hides,
wolf fur–ruffled hood.

Now, the housemistress thumps her foot
to snapping sticks and crackling flames.

Place your benedictions and blaspheme
mittens onto gasoline-soaked spruce.

Inhale the incense of scorched seal skin,
moose hide burning, porcupine quills

melting, and abalone shells surrendering
to seared salvation.

Deaf to what the children hear—
animal spirits igniting the sky.

She sees atonement; they see a funeral—
Little children marching toward the beach

in their final dress parade.

Vivian Faith Prescott

Telling Bones

He was told
not to speak his language
sit up straight
pay attention
science had the answers
but he knew
Raven
had created the earth

He was told
assimilation through education
they rapped hard
his fingers stung
chalk dust mixed with tears
he wrote
100 times
I will not speak Tlingit

He was told
don't cry until you are alone
in his dreams
he still had long hair
wore his own clothes
ran with bare feet
instead of stuffing them into
white man's shoes

He was told
not to run away
they bound his arms and legs
made him stand
in the middle of the hall
until he fell
and they whipped him

He was told
to march, march

like little soldiers
they rang bells to tell him
when to get dressed
brush his teeth
wash his face

He was told
he'd be a good farmer
they taught him about cows
animals and plants he'd never seen
he was taught
to be a good Christian
and to follow their three Gods

He was told
they would educate him
send him home to his island
as a better man
But instead like the other
188 children
he defied them
and died

They buried him
beneath the
Chemawa dirt
along with the others
who weren't allowed to go home
even in death

But they could no longer tell him
not to speak his tongue
they hear his bones
cry out in Tlingit
ax̱ yakg̱wahéiyagu ch'a yeisú k̲udzitee
my spirit lives

The-Place-for-Hunting-Snowy-Owls

I.

I imagine the little boy is learning the world was created
in seven days. He learns history begins with a man named
Columbus. He learns his heroes are Paul Revere, George
Washington, and Thomas Jefferson. He asks teacher why
no aunties are mentioned in books—he's laughed at. At lunch,
he eats their stale bread but he has sneaked some dry fish
into his pocket. He wishes he had seal grease to dip it in.
He learns Alaska was "discovered" by someone with a name
he cannot pronounce. He learns the Russians once "owned"
Alaska and were fools for selling it. He itches at his clothing
and fidgets in too tight shoes. He turns toward Raven rapping
at the frosted window and realizes this school must be something
that trickster has orchestrated. He smiles and struggles with
words on the page.

II.

In his dorm room, he tries to make sense of a map he borrowed
from the library. He traces the mountains with an owl feather
he keeps hidden in his Bible. This is Raven's world, but he misses
the sound of the snowy owl's shriek and hiss, the clapping beak,
the *hooo-uh, hooo-uh, hooo-uh, whu-whu-whu*. He thought he
could walk back home, even in winter. He's from *Ukpiagvik*,
The-Place-for-Hunting-Snowy-Owls. It's just over these mountains,
he thinks. He'll be cold in these clothes because the headmistress
burned his hand-made parka, his *qusruffaq*, the one Grandmother
made him before coming to this school.

III.

Three other students enter his dorm room. One is Tlingit,
one is Tsimshian, the other is Haida. They ask what he's doing.
He's packing his bag. He tells them he's going home because
he's sick of it here. He's been here several years and he's a
young man now. He can fend for himself back in his village.
They laugh and he laughs with them. They explain they are on
an island and he can't go over the mountains.

IV.

His friends tell him they're going to a meeting held behind
closed doors. No one is to know. At the meeting, they say how
they're graduating soon. They talk about organizing to get rid
of places like this. They say they want to be able to sit in any
seat at the movie theater. They want to go into any restaurant.
They say it's time to unite all Natives. So they meet again
and again and plan. They are the future of the Alaska Native
Brotherhood—the ANB.

V.

The boy still has four more years here at the boarding school.
He must sit and wait like the snowy owl waits for its prey.
He dreams of flying over the tundra, his wings beating the
familiar rhythm of the up-stroke and down-stroke. Below him,
the sedge meadows, lemmings, a whalebone arch.

II.

The first step toward civilization, toward teaching the Indians their mischief and folly of continuing in their barbarous practices, is to teach them the English language.

   —House Executive Document No. 1, 50th Congress, 1887

Haa toowú kei gux̱latseen a tin haa yoo x̱'atángi.

We gain strength of mind with our language.

   —Unidentified speaker, 1899 speech in Tlingit, in Sitka, Alaska (from *Haa Tuwunáagu Yis, for Healing Our Spirit*)

Wash Day

Every day was wash day.
—Grandma Jenny, Tlingit elder

When she was a girl, she spoke her language
and tasted soap, but now that she's old,
she says, everyone wants to know

her Lingít language. The school pays her
to remember laundered letters, knowledge
she's kept folded away as treasured blankets—

the Raven's tail and Chilkat. She's been trying
to wash away the English, soap forced
between her teeth, but the grit still lingers.

She looks away as she tries to explain how
to speak over a point of land—
x'aakanáx yoo x'atánk, meanings

we don't understand; tlél haa daa yaa ḵushugé.
Sometimes, she shakes out her old wool blanket,
fibers unloosening scraps of schoolhouse chalk.

With the red welt ache still stinging her fingers,
she hands her granddaughter the fifty dollar bill
in the envelope that the school gave to her.

Language Development

Our voice will always be heard in our land.
—Joe Wright, *Aanti Yéili*, Tlingit elder

I.

Back before the land-claims, her father called himself
an "Indian" so for years I taught that word to my daughter
and after the land claims we were told to say
Native.
So every once in a while she still says "Indian"
and then covers her mouth. "Does that mean
that once in a while I'm still an Indian?"

II.

We all flunked the third grade spelling test:
Klingket
Klingit
Thlingit
Thlinget
Words we couldn't spell because there was nowhere to read
about the real us because we are an oral culture whose words
are lobtailing on the Diving-Whale robe and circling in the
updraft of the Blanket-Above-All-Others. *Koloosh,*
the Russians called us and we said, Hell No, take back your name.

III.

Now, we pronounce our name with a voiceless L
Well, the linguists call it a voiceless L, but if you listen
closely, you can still hear us talking back.

IV.

They sent my daughter to the speech therapist
who pressed her lips together, making her form
labial letters: P-B-M, vibrations never felt before.
They told me she had trouble saying her THs
and Ls correctly. LLLLLLLLLL-all that air moving
through, spitting her ancestors out from the sides of her mouth.

V.

The teachers came to visit our homes in order to listen to our
grandmothers and when the grandmothers invited them inside
the teachers sat and stared, watching the larynx dance and tongues
contort, convincing themselves that our grandmothers were the
source of their difficulties teaching the children to pronounce
English letters. They tried to instruct us about the way we were
supposed to talk but we've been listening to their talk-talk-talk-talk
for a long time now and they still don't make any sense.

VI.

The Spanish High School class says, *Gracias*, thanks for the money.
The French High School class says, *Merci*, thanks for the money.
The imaginary-hopeful-non-existent Tlingit language High School class
says *Adoo sáwé Daana?* Where's the money?

VII.

Now that my daughter's grown, she teaches white folks how
to make those funning sounding letters, say their Ls correctly,
spittle dripping from the sides of their mouths. Sometimes, though,
she has to jump up on their dry tongues and dance around singing
her own vocables, *Yaw héi ya éi hi yaw aayáa, hu héi ya éi hi yaw aayáa,*
Yaw héi ya éi hi yaw aayáa, hu héi ya éi hi yaw aayáa.

English Lessons

These are the words from my children's English Phrase Book

repeat-after-me
repeat-after-me

Gee, your son is dark.
She looks like a little Indian baby?
What a cute Eskimo you are.
A Kling what?

repeat-after-me
repeat-after-me

You look exotic— what kind of person are you?
You don't look Indian to me.
How come you don't live on a reservation?
Can I touch your hair?

repeat-after-me
repeat-after-me

You're not Native enough.
There are only a few of us good Indians left.
How much Native are you?
Can I see your card?

repeat-after-me
repeat-after-me

repeat-after-me
repeat
after
me

Talk-Like-an-American

I wonder why ESL,
English-as-a-Second-Language classrooms
are filled with our village kids

who speak with Tlingit accents? Children
whose first language *is* English,
children wondering why

they're with immigrant kids from Russia,
Guatemala, and Thailand.

Children, en-un-ci-ate your words
and use your lips. Don't rock your letters
back and forth, halt those tones going up and down,

stop that sing-song sound. Quit that village-speech,
remove that tongue
from the roof of your mouth.

They are the "experts"
who don't understand the point
of our formation recedes

inside our throats to another generation,
sounds still resonating from the backs
of our mouths—wavelengths

felt across muskeg
in movements of muscle fibers,
a storied cycle thick across our papillae.

Yet, still our kids fill up ESL classrooms
making them talk-like-an-American.

And they keep on devising what they believe
are innovative methods, unaware
we've lived these same schemes before,

yet they keep on trying
like their forbearers did, keep on trying—
to thin out our tongues.

The Last Word

Chief Marie Smith Jones, The-Sound-that-Calls-People-From-Afar,
"With her death, the Eyak language becomes extinct."
    —Michael Krauss, 2008, in reference to the death of Chief
    Marie Smith Jones, *The-Sound-that-Calls-People-From-Afar*

Marie, when you were the last speaker
of your language left on this earth—

and you were dying—what words did you
cry out? What words did you speak

as the blanket drew closer, your forehead
cooled by cloth to your grooved brow,

your lips dampened with water; when heads
gathered near to hear your final words.

What was it you said as your mouth parted,
as air moved over parched lips?

You murmured in your language, word-strung
patterns like a fern's pinnae, your story stratum

uncurling time from this earth. And at once
you were there, Marie, with your clan members,

riding the boat downriver, arriving at the shore
where salmon greeted you—thick and red.

Together you gathered cockles and bird eggs,
built your first houses out of branches,

told stories of lake dwarfs, giant rats,
and a woman who married an octopus.

These things you whispered to us on the day
the ferns unfurled, when the air ceased

stirring about your room, when we leaned in
to hear your last words—
"This is when we became the Eyak."

III.

If we expect to infuse into the rising generation the leaven of American citizenship, we must remove the stumbling blocks of language.
                    —House Executive Document No. 1, 50th Congress, 1887

Haa yoo x'atángi haa at.óowux sitee. Kínde kei tutí.
Our language is our *at.óow.* Let's raise it up.
                    —Bessie Cooley, Tlingit elder, Teslin First Nation

Struggling with My Language

To my daughter, Yéilk', Cute Little Raven, who struggles with her
Tlingit language

Release me from my tongue—wedged hard
on the roof of my mouth.

I want letters to flow across my palate,
taste their colors of turquoise, red, and black.

I long to make the sounds of X', G,
undulating within my larynx—exhaled,

pinched, and tonal, the same letters I hear
in Raven's breath as he perches on a wire

beside my house, cawing, cawing.
And in the language of the eagle, circling,

waiting for speakers—tradition bearers
to tread outside of comfort zones

and assimilation to speak the language
of my elders. I long to clear myself of hesitant

words, spit out white, bland letters prattling
across my vocal folds, letters shoved down

generations ago. So I close my eyes,
and listen to the elders speak,

telling stories while their letters roll
and click on their tongues with such ease

in their guttural and pinching sounds—sounds
so familiar, but I am unable to journey back

inside my own mouth, knowing the memories
of language still lodge there,

resonating deep inside my throat.

Tight Tongues and Open Spaces

A closed mouth, index finger
to lips, downcast glance,

and flushed cheeks
are as much about language

as the words we use to fill
a grease dish.

Our mouths stretch to release,
but our hollows still wail.

Our faces are streaked
black, because we can't yet tell

our elder's cultural pause—
from the space where her grief resides.

Vivian Faith Prescott

Cephalic Index

I took my baby
to the Public Health Nurse
and the nurse measured her head,
pulling the tape taut around
my baby girl's thick black hair,
measuring her cranial capacity,
measuring,
measuring again just to be sure.
They wanted me to come back
but I told them
of course she has a family head,
she's from the Head House
—*Kaa Shaayi Hít,*
and she is also a Mork
She is Norwegian
She is *Táax'*—Snail
She is *Yéil*—Raven
But they made me
bring her back anyway
and they still kept measuring,
telling me they were concerned
about the diagnosis behind
the circumference of her head,
but I told them
no need to be concerned because
I am the mother-expert
who knows
there needs to be room enough
inside her head
for all our histories;
because someday I know she'll be the one—
the one who tells our stories,
since we belong
to a people
who are measured
by our words.

The Give and Taking of Names

The Removal

They gave our mountains, rivers, and lakes colonizer's names;
never asked what we called them, and if they did, they figured
they couldn't learn to pronounce them anyway; or maybe
they supposed, since there were no buildings, roadways, and schools,
there were no names.

Restore

A century later they're taking our old and honored names—
good enough now—tagging them to tourist ventures: cabin rentals,
fishing charters, a bear zoo, and eco-tours.

Sensibility

Maybe they think, after two hundred years, our names are void of meaning,
after all they've made sense of eating on Oneida dishes, driving
Cherokee cars, and walking on Mohawk carpets.

Vivian Faith Prescott

Lingít Language Extinction

He goes to school
and they talk to him
in English and
he reads in English
and he eats
hamburgers, fries, and
drinks Coca-Cola
for lunch and
he goes home
to watch TV
and at dinner he talks
with his parents in English
and his grandmother calls him
and she speaks into the phone in English
and he goes to bed at night
and in his dreams

he is silent.

IV.

This language, which is good enough for a white man and a black man, ought to be good enough for the red man.

— House Executive Document No. 1, 50th Congress, 1887

At yáa awunéiyi een yéi x'ayaká.

— *Koolyéik*

Say it with respect.

— Roby Littlefield, *Koolyéik*,
Cultural Archives Specialist, Tlingit Language Instructor

Traditions

For my daughter, Brea

In midwinter's den, I nursed my bear cub
       during Winter-Black-Bear-Month:
       When-Cubs-are-Born-in-the-Den.

I named her Winter-Black-Bear-Woman,
       S'eek Taakw Shaawát, a name too long,
       unsuitable for blank lines, but fitting

according to Lingít elder-women
       huffing their warm breath to catch her scent—
       essence of lineage on the island of bears

from a bear mother—born with small eye-slits
       and thin skin, unable to read letters
       on the pages of fairy tales and schoolbooks.

Experts tell me she's illiterate
       like her father, yet she reads the hollows
       of sandpiper tracks on mudflats,

white blossoms dotting thimbleberry bushes,
       the silver flash of salmon, and knows
       what the elders tell us is true—

in February, her birth month, the black bear mother
       emerges briefly from hibernation,
       pushing her cubs out in the snow,

rolling them around like our women once did,
       bathing children in seawater—
       And two hundred years later,

daughters and black bears still plait this memory
       —the nip of the sea's sting
       and ice shards woven in new fur.

Vivian Faith Prescott

Know My Skin

To know my skin, smell bull kelp
and popweed, catch my scent

after a morning walk on the beach.
Know my skin—pronounce my name,

your voice rising and falling; don't laugh
whenever I speak. Be able to lick

the bark of my skin, at s'*áxt*—it tastes
like soggy earth, the flavor of rainforest.

And listen—don't be offended
by scratchy sounds, settle in among

silences. Know my skin—look beyond
paleness, see reindeer herds,

glaciers calving, kittiwakes sitting
on drifting logs, and snails. Learn

my outer shell, *ax daakanóox'u;*
understand my membrane-layered world;

touch peculiar stories, become familiar
with strangeness: my antenna eyestalks,

the spiral of my shell, and my slick-
tongued foot.

Your Emergence

I floated your tiny body in the ocean
above sea anemones and bull kelp,

a taste of saltwater to your lips. I placed you
on the shore where barnacles scraped

your feet, popweed burst between your toes,
let you eat a fist full of goose tongue.

In the woods we ate spruce tips, dug
licorice roots, peeled salmonberry shoots

and unfolded new ferns. I chewed the land up
in offering to you, a bundle inside your mouth,

set you down and you crawled in dirt,
pulling grass, feeling gummy alder leaves,

licking soil and stones. It's then that I knew
you were ready to surface into this world

tasting the words like the tang on our skins—
wet-sticky-salty-gritty—alive.

Vivian Faith Prescott

Creating the Sacred

For Cute Little Raven, my daughter

Some of our clothes are considered sacred,
haa at.óowu—cedar-carved hats, woven
robes, button blankets, and deer-hide tunics,

sacrificed objects dance around our bodies.
And I see you, daughter, how you began
in your diapered bottom, padding

across the floor, slipping baby-feet into
your father's rubber boots.
Today, you wear your girlfriend's shoes,

my shirt, your stepdad's pants, grandfather's
hat, and a ring your father gave me
when I was just fifteen. Every day the bend

of your knee and sway of your arm dances
in the ceremony of the ordinary.
Yet, I know for you these clothes are no longer

"play-things" for dressing up—*ash kawdliyát naa.ádi*.
They've become your *at.óow*,
your grandparent-mother-father-sister scents,

seeping between synthetic and cotton
threads, creating the sacred—the moment
the oils from their skin meets with yours.

Tundatáan yák'w (little face of thought)

○

Shéiyi yahaayí,
Xáanaa chéx'i wé dei káx'
Sigóowu júkkx'

Shadow of a spruce,
evening's shadows on the trail
happy robins

○

Yéil wakhéeni,
Haa gaaxdaasheeyí áyá
Shtax'héen taak

Raven's tears,
this is our cry song
in the Bitter Water River

○

Shawátshaan Kées',
l'ein héeni táakx' yéi yatee wé nées'
du yáa ayagoonéi

Old Tide Woman,
the sea urchin lives in the tide pool
respect her

Tundatáan yák'w (little face of thought)

○

tleilóo kíji wé,
ḵ'eikaxwéin kayáani woogaaxí
aẖ sée ẖ'usyée

The moth's wings,
flower petals crying
under my daughter's feet

○

ayakayadán ḵa
du ts'ootaan shíyi wé t'sítskw wooshee,
du jaají sheeyí

It's snowing heavy and
the songbird sings her morning song,
her snowshoe song

○

Gáas' tayee áwé
yoo aan ka.á wooshee,
yá tl'átk yéigi

Beneath the house post
the earthquake sings,
this soil spirit

V.

The instruction of the Indians in their vernacular is not only of no use to them, but is detrimental to the cause of their education and civilization.

> — J. D. C. Atkins, commissioner, *Annual Report of the Commissioner of Indian Affairs*, 1887

Ch'a uwayáa du yoo x̱'atángi haa séix̱ aawayeeshée yáx̱ yatee yá x'óow.
> —G̱ooch Ooxú

It is as if his words are like a robe pulled over our shoulders, a strength-giving robe.

> —Richard King, G̱ooch Ooxú

Disturbing the Tourists at Glacier Bay National Park Lingít Language Immersion Camp

> *Yá xáanaa áwé áa yoo s$\underline{x}$'asatángin.*
> —*Tóok'*

> *This evening, the dancers gave it voice.*
> —Charlie Jim, *Tóok'*

Yes, we were being loud—loud enough
for our grandparents to hear us
across Icy Strait, atop Mount Fairweather.

Loud enough to calve the ice
and disturb the tourists who leaned
against our fine white tablecloths,

pale hands lifting silver forks,
dining on halibut, salmon, and crab.
Above them, floorboards creaked,

weighted by our old bones; rafters
hummed with voices. They dabbed
their mouths with green cloths,

and patted their chests to break
the congestion of strange drums.
The waiter informed us, *You're disturbing*

the tourists with all this dancing
and singing. And like their grandfathers,
they assumed if they couldn't see us,

couldn't hear us, we'd just go away.
So they sat pleased in the silence,
licking salmon scales from their knives.

Vivian Faith Prescott

I Know There Is a Name for You

For Duffy

I walk along the path
following the ancient curve of shore
at *Sít' Eetí Geey* beneath
the alder and cottonwoods
summer's age. I see you waddling
and my first thought is how Raven
fashioned your quills from yellow cedar,
and I marvel at the many shades of brown
moving with the sway of your shape.
They catch the light—quills making patterns
like moccasin tops across your back.
I think of the grandmothers' methods
of collecting quills, how the old ones
would throw a blanket covering you,
and from beneath you'd shuffle
leaving us a gift of sewing needles and earrings.

Yet here you are giving me a gift: the mere sight of you.
So I do not mean to be rude,
but I have left the Lingít noun-book in my room
and all I can say is
ch'a aadei yéi xat na.oo.
Please forgive me,
Porcupine, please forgive me
for I do not know your name.

Glacier Bay Belonging

People at *Chookán*, spirits of Woman-In-the-Ice, a girl overcome by
shifting ice destroying their village. How we belong to a place, place
belongs to us—Belonging to People-of-the-Iceberg, belonging to story—
a friend devoured by a bear, his remains, like us, scatter from here; to
my children, whose auntie drowned in the shadow of Ground-Squirrel
Mountain; to uncle and cousin who rode the tidal wave in *Ltu.áa* Bay
over an island and lived; to those on this beach recalling ceremony,
offering food to the fire for our women murdered last year; to the elder
hunter who mourns the loss of his hunting grounds; to the *Chookaneidí*
man arrested for shooting a sacred seal intended for the ceremony
to honor our dead—Now *Sit' Eetí G̲eey*, the bay, belongs to campers,
cruisers, and kayakers, who purchase their belongings—red T-shirt, ball
cap, and plastic water bottle, engraved with an inscription claiming
they've been to a place where they cannot pronounce our names: *S'é
Shuyee, X̲áat Tú, Sit' Eetí G̲eey*, the place where cracking ice and seal
yaps echo in the spaces   of all our hushed
belongings.

Vivian Faith Prescott

Receiving Your Name at Glacier Bay

To my daughter, Cháas' Koowú Tláa
        —Mother-of-Humpy-Tail

Today, you've been given
your great auntie's name, meaning

"the force compelling humpy salmon
to return to the stream."

The fish always loved her scent
and came back again and again,

as you now call auntie every summer
back to the Alsek River,

the place where she tipped over
in her skiff and drowned,

she returns again—woman
with a wide-open-legged-spread,

hands in water, waving fins past her thighs.

Angoon Harvest Pantoum

Tongues unable to wrap around words
as easy as pulling apart hot-oiled bannock;
quiet elders laugh and then don't laugh
as words sugar over bowls of berries.

Oiled-hot bannock pulls apart easily
as we sit at tables trimming beach greens,
while berries sugar over bowls of words,
purple buckets and scissors in hand.

Beach greens on tables are trimmed where we sit.
The elders don't laugh and then laugh quiet.
In their hands, plastic buckets and purple scissors.
In their hands, words, our tongues
            are unable to wrap around.

Vivian Faith Prescott

Filling My Basket

We tléi<u>k</u>w <u>x</u>oo
a<u>x</u> toowú sigóo
      kanat'á
      tleikatánk
      was'x'aan tléigu
haat tán we kaltásk
      a<u>x</u> toowú sigóo.

Among the berries
my spirit is happy
      blueberries
      red huckleberries
      salmonberries
Bring the berry basket here
      My spirit is happy.

VI.

Every nation is jealous of its own language, and no nation ought to be more so than ours...to the perfection of its people. True Americans.
      —J. D. C. Atkins, commissioner,
      Annual Report of the Commissioner of Indian Affairs, 1887

Haa ḵusteeyí yeenáax' áwé has shakawligaa.
      —Kinchnáalx̱

Our culture is draped upon our bodies.
      —George Davis, Kinchnáalx̱

Report on Indian Education, October, 1889
Washington, D.C., and Juneau, Alaska, 2003

These are the General Principals for a system of Education
says Commissioner of Education Thomas J. Morgan,
October 1889, gave the same speech then as he gave today
when he walked into the twenty-first century and saw my daughter
sitting in the back of her high school classroom.

He said—whatever steps are necessary, under any circumstances
education is the Indians' only salvation. They will become
honorable-useful-happy citizens in a great republic
sharing all its blessings.

And when he left the class and walked down the hall,
he was shaking a can of red spray paint, handed it to a white kid
who sprayed KAN—Kill All Natives all over town; painted it
in the middle of the road and stained it on the rock bluffs
like a pictograph announcing the Indians' only salvation.

And there were board meetings, newspaper articles
town assemblies, public testimony and everyone said—
       whatever steps are necessary education is the Indians'
       only salvation. They will become honorable-useful-happy citizens
       in a great republic sharing all its blessings.

Vivian Faith Prescott

No Heroes

For D. W.

I'm *Superman*, the child said,
looking at me with his narrow
wide-set eyes, flashing brown-

stained teeth, scraping his chair
sideways, then back again,
hopping his butt up and down.

It was my first day in class
and I, too, was learning
his language;

I was to teach color words
and animal nouns, and I tried
to pronounce the word

for red: <u>x</u>'*aan*—but he told me,
    You're saying it wrong,
and I understood that he meant

<u>x</u>'*aan*—color and fire pulsing through
half his veins, the metal-scent
of his mother, the scuff of amber

glass bottles across the kitchen
floor, the silk red cape draping
the couch, the loaded rifle
rusting in the corner.

Traveling in Circles at the Local Video Store

We must not be traveling
in the same social circles,

the older woman said to me,
because I haven't seen you
around town.

I try not to laugh, but I laugh
anyway, telling her I'm learning
Tlingit oratory—

Did you hear the story
about Raven and the Tides?

About the Tlingit version
of the Battle of Sitka?

She looks at me with a face
that says *I thought I knew you,*
but now, do I know you?

And I know she's gauging
the shade of my skin. I know

the question is coming, but *how*
it comes I can't tell, not certain

if it'll be wide eyes with raised
eyebrows, the eyes noting

the flakes of brown on my nose
or the blues in my irises.

So I say something to her in Lingít
and there's a Tlingit girl

behind the counter listening to us,
and giggles at my words,

bringing this young girl's circle closer
to mine and the older woman

is silent now still trying to figure out
why I am talking in circles

when I tell her about the recent clan
conference here in town:

Tlingits, Haidas, and Tsimshians
gathering; academics, elders,

and students sharing knowledge. I tell her
how *Yaakwdáat's* ptarmigan song

is still dancing in my head.
But she never even noticed

three hundred Natives walking
around town telling stories.

The older woman remains speechless,
time hangs waiting for me to fill it in

until I say, *I guess we don't travel
in the same circles.*

She says nothing and turns from us,
while the Tlingit girl and I,

our lives still circling each other,
talk about words and our elder's

new grandchild, the one they
gave a Tlingit name.

And I turn around, wondering
if the other woman will ever want

to step into our circle, but I don't
think so because I saw that when

she departed our conversation,
heading for the door—she was still

walking her straight line.

Vivian Faith Prescott

Rising

To Dick and Nora

Gaydanaak̲

Haa daadéi woosh kaanáx̲ gayda.á
k̲a haa x̲'éide k̲unayis.aax̲
haa dachx̲ánx̲' i yan
yeetusix̲án
        haa toowú k̲ilgéi
            Gaydanaak̲
Gunalchéesh adaanáx̲ yeeydinaagi
yá Lingít K̲usteeyí yis.

Gather around us, you all
and listen to us
our grandchildren.
We love you all,
      We are proud
         Stand up
Thank you for rising through it
for this Tlingit way of life.

VII.

The tribal relations should be broken up…and the individual substituted.
           —Thomas J. Morgan
           Commissioner of Indian Affairs, 1889

Yá Lingit'aaní geix' woosh jin toolshát yeisú.
           —*Katyé*

In this world, we're still holding each other's hands.
           —David Kadashan, *Katyé,* Tlingit elder

Annie

Do you have dry fish?
Her native spirit cries,
every day,
always forgetting
that she is locked here
forced to eat
pork chops and green beans.

Where's my seaweed?
She spits her snuff in the hall
in the ghostly spittoon in the corner.

Intolerable behavior.

So she begs for more.
 My tummy hurts—
No good white man food.
And she is given
pork chops and green beans.

Do you have herring eggs?
I say "No *shaawát.*"
And she kisses me
after hearing her native tongue.

Someone put her here
and took away her life,
and took away her food.
So she died quietly one evening
after being given a meal
of pork chops and green beans.

Vivian Faith Prescott

We Who Are Tlingit: *Lingitx̱ Haa Sitee*

Even speech at a distance becomes one with someone.
— A. P. Johnson, *Íx̱t'ik' Éesh*, Sitka, 1971

Aaá,
yéi áyá ax̱ tuwatee.
Lingitx̱ haa sateeyí,
yóo yee yax̱wsikaa
át ḵuwaháa yeedát
yeedát
i sé gas.aax̱—
x̱'anidataan.

Haa Léelku hás,
Haa Shagoon
kei haa toowú yeeysigít.
Ách áwé
ldakát uháan toowú wlitseen.
tlél toox̱éx'w,
yaa x̱'antudatán haa yoo x̱'atángi.

Yes,
This is how I feel.
We who are Tlingit,
I am saying to you
it is time for it
right now,
let them hear your voice—
speak.

Our grandparents,
our ancestors
you awakened our spirit.
That is why
we have gained strength of mind.
We are not sleeping;
we are speaking our language.

Role Model

You
unknowable clanned
impossibly figured
      seventeen-inch waist
          no boobs
               no sex
five-inch-long footed
      high-heeled woman
      from the Northwest coast
      with Down-South Native clothes
      and Inupiat mukluks

whose gift box says
you play a traditional Inuit game
and originate from the Totem Pole People
and are able to speak the Lingít language
with your plastic tongue—

My little girl
is combing
her dreams through your hair
and dancing around
our living room
singing the Disney
Pocahontas song.
How am I supposed to tell her
that she will never become
a Tlingit Barbie doll?

Vivian Faith Prescott

Whisper To the Baby

For Grandmothers

I whisper in the baby's ear
sweet Lingít words—

Ixsixán,
chxánk'—
i likoodzí.
Ax x'éit sa.áx.
yaadú i léelk'w sháa,
Kinees.aax,
Kinees.aax.

I love you
my grandchild—
you are amazing.
Listen to me.
Here is your grandmother,
listen,
listen.

Sociology 101

For Yéilk' and L.T. S.

My daughter flunked Sociology 101,
told the teacher that violence in Alaska

wasn't related to the consumption
of ice cream—violence was her relation.

She was told she didn't have a *society*
only a *culture* as if a hierarchy of terms.

I tell her, maybe they think you don't
have a society because you drive a Toyota,

and you buy smoked fish at Jerry's Meats,
and your regalia is your Carhartts

and a silver labret pierced below your
lower lip. She finished the course not knowing

what *sociology* really means, said she tried
to look it up, said Webster was a white guy

so what does he know about clans and houses,
names, laws, taboos, and *at.óow,*

those unseen things, Lingít sociological terms
absent in pale textbook pages. And like the

revolutionary she is, she handed the instructor
a gift—a book explaining how to decolonize

their methodologies, and walked away wearing
her failing grade as a badge of dissent,

a letter in the colonizer's language meaning
you still don't know what *sociology* means,

meaning you still don't know how to assimilate,
meaning you are still resisting. Us.

VIII.

The people of the State of Alaska find that English is the common unifying language of the State of Alaska and the United States of America, and declare a compelling interest in promoting, preserving, and strengthening its use.
> —Section 1, Ballot Measure 6
>
> (Alaskans approved the initiative statute on November 3, 1998, by a sixth-nine percent to thirty-one percent vote)

Aaa, has du x̱'éidei gax̱du.áax̱.
> —K̲aal.átk'

Yes, it will be heard from their lips.
> —Charlie Joseph, K̲aal.átk', Tlingit Elder

Shades of Meaning

I.

What kind of name is that? they said.
How dare they give that baby a Lingít name?
A given name written right on their birth certificate
one meaning—strength
one meaning—faith
another meaning—amazing

II.

In response:
Well, how dare we make you pronounce
a name with a voiceless *L*
and click your letter sharply
in the middle of a word.
We challenge you to speak
our names aloud,
discover the shades of meaning
behind our house screens,
the fire pit burning
in the center of planked floor,
children still dancing
as killer whales through gyre.

Vivian Faith Prescott

Yéil Tundatáani, Raven Thinking

To Richard Dauenhauer, Xwaayeenák

Sometime this morning, I was unable
to prevent skin-shifting from lips to beak,

while saying aloud an English word,
using Lingít pronunciations.

And I laughed at myself realizing
Raven pesters my vernacular, that old trickster

hopping his mayhem dance—creating
code switching in the midst of my brain.

Tlingit Oratory

> *Let the voice of your toenails be heard.*
>> —Clarence Jackson, *Galtín, Asx'áak, Daa naawú,*
>> *Tá Gooch*

Let the voice of your toenails be heard
clacking on planked floors,
sound seeping into cedar-whorled wood.

Yet in response to your oratory,
your words—like claps of thunder
searching for a mountainside,
skip across linoleum floors
and hang upon aluminum-frame windows
and spackled walls.

And here I sit in the back row
with those who understand the protocol—
we stomp our feet
and watch the deaf ones
unable to hear our voices,
because they're still clapping with their hands.

Vivian Faith Prescott

The Weight of Language

The elder reads a passage of Lingít oratory
and I close my eyes
to listen
slowly lowering
a 16 oz. lead
tied to liter
spinning hook and line
sinking
down
to
sea floor
moving through kelp bed
this salinity
suspended
inside her phonetic
in utero.

Post 9/11 Airport Pantoum

To my niece who was profiled at SeaTac Airport after 9/11

They took the dark-skinned girl away,
held her against her will in an interrogation room.
No profiling, they said, but what nation are you from?
In her traditional language she told them
          she was a frog who came downriver under ice.

So the interrogators held her will against the room.
And she tried to explain how she was created twice:
          First from a rock and then a leaf;
that the frog on the ice flowed down
          with her language beneath the river.
Instead they listed her risk factor as trickster.

So first she created a rock and two leaves,
then let loose one hundred twenty thousand no-fly feathers,
in order to trick the risk they hadn't factored in
and fly off with her own nation left blank
          and unchecked inside a box.

But as a hundred twenty thousand no-fly feathers loosened
the trickster, risking all they'd factored;
from their box, they blanked out their own nation
          and departed unchecked,
taking the girl's dark skin along with them.

Vivian Faith Prescott

Paper Rooms

You say you were offended
when you stepped inside my poem,
beside my character who spoke Lingít

properly as she was educated to do—
a way to identify herself. Raven woman
stands accused of being unidentifiable

because you cannot tell her skin color
from someone in a warring country
or her language from the enemy's.

You're slighted by the disrespect,
by language spoken in the room—a room
filled with paper and font

where a woman identifies herself—as a frog,
before she calls herself an "American."
You are in this room alongside strange words,

underlines and apostrophes expressing
our idioms, forgetting the five hundred nations
conversing before your very own.

So I wrote the poem in English, *your* language,
in order for you to be disturbed about
how Ravens figure in this outlandish world.

If my words offend, would you step outside
on your porch, read the poem aloud?
You can do this in your own language

and if you need—you can borrow mine.
I want you to hear your own words raucous,
then spin and turn to dive.

Speak-speak, speak-speak, release the words—
loosen them from your vocabulary; untidy your room,
open wide and escape them

animate from your mouth. Now, hear the voice
of the character in my poem, experience
the ruler slapped on her grandmother's hands,

a mouth full of soap; sense the door closing,
feel the dignity when you utter your defiance
aloud. Here, I say again, like I wrote in the poem

Ch'a aadei yéi xat na.oo—Please forgive me
if you misunderstand the meaning in this room—

frogs hopping over tone marks, ice sloughing off
riverbanks, the flutter of wings at your door.

IX.

Some of their languages weren't even written. If we want to have all the Native people stay in the villages the rest of their lives, that's fine, but times have changed.

—Susan Fischetti, official spokesperson,
Alaskans for a Common Language, 1999

I sé gas.aax. Lingít x'éináx sá.
—Keixwnéi ka Xwaayeenák

Let them hear you voice. Say it in Lingít.
—Nora, Keixwnéi, and Richard, Xwaayeenák Dauenhauer,
Tlingit Language Scholars

Mocking Talking

Do not swallow the root juice
that I'm writing about
a cat-o'-nine-tailed history,

the knotted thong and cotton-
plaited cord, the language thieves' cat,
stinging back to high-collared days,

in the only way I can, with the words
of those who bent us over and flogged
our tongues.

But really, I say it's only Raven's
forked talons clutching my own tongue
when I should have roots

protruding in every direction,
and Raven letting loose my tongue
when I should let have let Muta hold it.

It's Raven throwing pinecones
against my head, crooning his soft
hollowed hoot,

reminding me, every time I speak
the colonizers' words,
I, too, am calling out to death.

Vivian Faith Prescott

Preservation Blues

Sitting in the language classroom
four white faces
staring back at me
four white faces
staring back at me
sing it Corporation
sing it Preservation
four white faces staring back at me

Walking in the grocery store
four white words
repeated back to me
four white words
repeated back to me
sing it Corporation
sing it Preservation
four white words repeated back to me

Driving by the road signs
four white names
looking out at me
four white names
looking out at me
sing it Corporation
sing it Preservation
four white names looking out at me

Visiting the classroom
four white teachers
hiding our curriculum
four white teachers
hiding our curriculum
sing it Corporation
sing it Preservation
four white teachers hiding our curriculum

Sing it Corporation
Sing it Preservation
Corporation—the same white word repeated back to me
         the same white word repeated back to me
Preservation—hiding our road signs while looking to me
         hiding our road signs while looking to me

Vivian Faith Prescott

Saliva

Saliva fills and seeps
from the sides of my tongue

as I form the voiceless *L*.
I know when I'm speaking

correctly because elders tell me
I should be spitting when I talk.

Sometimes, I chew a piece of candy,
keeping it soft and pliable,

sticking it to the roof of my mouth,
my glands salivating, making sounds

once exotic to my ear, practiced
two years before I got it right.

Now, I suck on glottal letters,
scraping air sopped in serous

and mucous, my moist
homily, because

for generations our mouths
were only familiar with cracks

in our nippled buds, and the hard
packed dust of our own red clay.

The Linguist

He wanted to teach me about tall grass
and icebergs, the first time I saw him
on the beach at *Xunaa*,

as if he'd been waiting for me to listen
to his tutorial. He wanted to instruct me
with his allegories,

teach me about rocks and ravens.
But I wanted free morphemes, fixed words,
something tangible

and arranged in time, so I could fit
my fossilized terms—things I already knew—
into his puzzled worldview.

So, I cut the conversation short, passed
on his sage instruction until I noticed him,
this time in Totem Park,

Sheet'ká kwáan. I didn't marvel at him
sitting on the water-sogged log. I looked him
in the eye and said *Wáa sá i yatee?*

He raised his head, opened his mouth wide,
and a sound emerged from his throat,
and I'm sure I heard

Tlél wáa sá. Wa.é ku.aa? but then again,
it could have been *caw, caw, caw, caw.*

Vivian Faith Prescott

Lingua Nullius

The bugle has sounded again
and you come rushing into our minds

trouncing upon unclaimed acres,
deciding we're incapable of abstract

thought: Our minds *tabula rasa,*
barren and waiting to be filled.

You see us void of meaning,
tongues without owners, like you

once saw our land—*Terra nullius.*
Well, if you perceive blankness—nothing—

then perhaps you may set up your pavilions
on our tongues; but know

that in our Lingít language
we cannot speak about body parts

without their owners being attached
to the noun—so you cannot

unfasten the stretch of our canvas
from the marrow of our hair—

and you cannot separate us from
the Lively-Frog-in-Pond or the Crying-for-Medicine.

Woman-with-Words

For Nora

<u>Keixwnéi</u>
I am telling your story now
because someday
you will have a thousand grandchildren.
Your books, your words
are our *at.óow*.
And someday our grandchildren
will ask to hear your story,
about the Woman-with-Words
and we will speak
your poems in Lingít,
tell traditional stories in Lingít,
sing in Lingít,
and we will be
your grandchildren dancing—
dancing with your words.

Vivian Faith Prescott

Backward Progression

Why all of a sudden, now, are they going backwards? Some of their languages weren't even written.

— Susan Fischetti, official spokesperson,
Alaskans for a Common Language, 1999

Because I want to speak my Native language,
you perceive me "going backwards."

Backward to where? Toward savageness
and barbarianism?

Well, I'm defying your linear march
up cement steps to your domed roofs,

     the back-and-forth
you call time and progress,
        the back-and-forth you call politics.

I defy your ballots and appeals, defining
the way I hold my teacup and saucer,

your belief in the melting pot, the notion
a common language gives us strength.

So I'm offering you a warning—listen
quietly. Listen, while your mind is asleep

in your hilltop tents, as candlelight
dims, as your words saturate the spaces

between your gray matter; when you can't
tell the direction of our voices,

how they murmur from the bushes,
with a wet hiss and jagged click,

sounds garbled—know it's only
our grandparents awakening. Listen

to our whispers' first meeting,
our hot breath folding into breath.

Listen for our tones rising, the footsteps
of scratchy throats—These will be our war cries
encircling your encampment.

Yáa yeedát a tóo haa kaawahayi ḵusti ách a x̱'éidáx̱ has ash kaawashéet' has du léelk'u hás aadéi ḵunoogu yé. Yeedát áwé ch'u oowayáa yú gaaw du.áx̱ji.

        —Ḵaal.átk'

And now this life we are in, it was this that removed from their mouths the things their grandparents used to do. And now it's just as if the drum is heard.

        —Charlie Joseph, Ḵaal.átk', Tlingit elder

Aaa,
Yéi áyá.
Gunalchéesh.

Yes,
this is it.
Thank you.

Tlingit Language Sound Charts

Lingít letter	*Lingít X̲'énáx̲* example word	English translation
.	wa.e/ naa.át	you/clothes
ch	cheech	porpoise
ch'	ch'áak'	bald eagle
d	dáa	weasel
dl	dleit	snow/white
dz	dzánti	flounder
g	gaaw	drum/time/bell/clock
g̲	g̲ooch	wolf
gw	a gwéinlí	hoof
g̲w	jig̲wéina	hand towel
h	héen	water
j	jánwu	mountain goat
k	kakéin	yarn
k'	k'ínk'	fermented fish heads
k̲'	k̲'eik̲'w	sea pigeon
kw	kwaan	smallpox
k'w	k'wát'	egg
k̲w	naak̲w	devil fish/octopus
k̲'w	k̲'wátl	pot
l	lóol	fireweed
l'	l'ook	coho/silver salmon
n	náayadi	partially dried salmon
s	séew	rain
s'	s'eek	black bear
sh	shaa	mountain
t	toowú	mind
t'	t'á	king salmon
tl	tléik'	no
tl'	tl'eex	garbage
ts	tsaa	seal
ts'	ts'ats'ée	small songbird
w	wasóos	cow
x	xóon	north wind
x'	x'áax'	apple
x̲	x̲áat	salmon
x̲'	x̲'áan	fire
xw	gáaxw	duck
x̲'w	x̲'éishxw	blue jay
x̲w	(du) húnx̲w	older brother
x̲'w	x̲'wáat	Dolly Varden/trout
y	yéil	raven

Lingít vowel	Lingít word	English definition	English example (sounds like)
a	at daayí	birch	America (low tone)
á	t'á	salmon (general)	America, was (high)
aa	aan	town/land	fall (low)
áa	áa	lake	fall (high tone)
e	dandewooyaa	marmot	elephant (low)
é	té	rock	pet (high tone)
ei	seit	necklace	gate (low tone)
éi	dléit	snow/white	vein (high)
i	Ginjichwáan	Canadian/British	hint (low)
í	hít	house	hit (high tone)
ee	ee ká	room	he (low tone)
ée	néech	shoreline	keep (high)
u	nukshiyáan	mink	bush (low)
ú	gút	dime	put (high tone)
oo	woosh yaayí	pair	glue (low)
óo	óonaa	gun	boot (high)

Notes

1   Foreword: Excerpt from "Perspectives of a Tlingit Language Instructor," *Sharing Our Pathways* 10.2 (March/April 2005): 13–15, and in Vivian (Martindale) Prescott, "Lingítx̱ Haa Sateeyí, We Who Are Tlingit: Contemporary Tlingit Identity and the Ancestral Relationship to the Landscape"(PhD diss., U of Alaska Fairbanks, 2007): 497–508.

8   "Invitation to Feast": K̲oo.éex̱' or k̲u.éex̱': Literally, "to invite people," a traditional Tlingit memorial ceremony. X̱áat: The word for salmon is formed in the back of the throat; X̱'éishx̱'w: "blue jay"; the letter x̱' is one of the most difficult letters in the Lingít language. A glottalized letter, uvular. Wolf and hill: G̲ooch, gooch. There's a slight difference in where the letter g is formed in the throat: X̱aat and x̱áat: Tree root and salmon, a difference in the tone of the vowel. S'eek (black bear) l'ook, and ch'áak'(eagle): Pinched sounds are indicated by an apostrophe and are made near the teeth.

14   "The-Place-for-Hunting-Snowy-Owls" is the traditional name for Barrow, Alaska.

17   "Wash Day": In Lingít, the word for metaphor is translated as "speaking over a point of land," which is a metaphor in itself.

31   "Know My Skin": ax daakanóox'u is a term meaning "outer shell" but means much more regarding Tlingit kinships.

34–35 *Tundatáan yák'w* (little face of thought): Lance Twitchell created a Tlingit word that serves as the Japanese word "haiku": *Tundatáan yák'w* (little face of thought). Gunalchéesh to X̱'unei (Lance Twitchell) a.k.a. Troubled Raven (*Sh tukawdlixéel'i Yéil*) and Sealaska Heritage Institute and for their Tlingit language dictionaries and Tlingit language lesson books.

38   "I know there is a name for you": Sit' Eetí G̲eey: Glacier Bay National Park, Place-where-the-glacier-was. Literally, Bay in the Glacier's imprint; x̱alak'lách' : Porcupine (x̱alak'ách'); ch'a aadei yéi x̱at na.oo: Please forgive me (singular).

46   "Traveling in Circles at the Local Video Store": Yaakw.daat: Yakutat, Alaska.

48, 51 "Rising" and "We Who Are Tlingit: Lingitx̱ haa sitee " : The Lingít language poems were fashioned from the syntax of elders' speeches and a study of poetics and language from various sources (see below) and from my own notes in order to hone my skills as a beginning speaker. Please forgive me for any grammatical or spelling mistakes.

54   "Sociology 101": Smith, Linda Tuhiwai, *Decolonizing Methodologies: Research and Indigenous Peoples* (London: Zed Books, 1999).

58 "Tlingit Oratory": Tlingit protocol instructs us to stomp our feet. Clarence Jackson told me that clapping of hands is a "Western" practice.

60 "Post 9/11 Airport Pantoum": Kaachx̱aana. áak'w is the Tlingit name for Wrangell, Alaska, and Shtax'héen Kwáan is "People of Bitter Water." Shtax'héen is "Bitter Water" or "Silty Water" (in English, Stikine River).

67 "The Linguist": Xooniyaa: Hoonah, Alaska; Sheet'ká kwaan: Sitka, Alaska; Wáa sá i yatee: How are you? Tléil wáa sá wáa eh ku. áa: I am fine and you?

68 "Lingua Nullius": Lively-Frog-in-Pond is a character in Tlingit oral traditions. Crying-for-Medicine is the name of an oral tradition featuring a specific medicine.

69 "Woman-with-Words": Nora Dauenhauer's poem, "Granddaughters Dancing," in *The Droning Shaman* (Haines, Alaska: Black Current Press, 1988):1–93.

During a language immersion retreat at Dog Point Fish Camp in Sitka, Alaska, Ethel Makinen, *Daasdiyáa*, and Irene Paul, *Yaax̱l.aat*, assisted with some of the quotations in this book. Language classes offered by Nora and Richard Dauenhauer through the University of Alaska Southeast assisted with explanations and translations.

Other language texts that provided assistance include Lance Twitchell, *Tlingit Dictionary* (draft version) (Juneau, AK: Troubled Raven Productions, n.d. Print). Richard Dauenhauer and Nora Dauenhauer, *Lingít X̱'éinax̱ Sá, Say it in Tlingit: A Tlingit Phrase Book* (Juneau, AK: Sealaska Heritage Institute, 2002. Print); Richard Dauenhauer and Nora Marks Dauenhauer, eds., *Haa Tuwunáagu Yís: For Healing Our Spirit, Tlingit Oratory* (Juneau, AK: Sealaska Heritage Institute, 1990. Print); Richard Dauenhauer and Nora Dauenhauer. *Beginning Tlingit* (Juneau, AK: Sealaska Heritage Foundation, 2000. Print); Richard Dauenhauer and Nora Dauenhauer, eds., *Because We Cherish You: Sealaska Elders Speak to the Future* (Juneau, AK: Sealaska Heritage Foundation, 1981. Print); Henry Davis, ed., *English/Tlingit Dictionary, Nouns* (Sitka, AK: Sheldon Jackson College, 1976. Print).

See Francis Paul Prucha, ed., *Documents of Indian Policy*, 2nd ed. (Lincoln: U of Nebraska P, 1990):1-396. Web. http://www.alaskool.org.

71 Closing quotation: Charlie Joseph speech from Dauenhauer and Dauenhauer, *Because We Cherish You* (1-77). Other quotation sources: Roby Littlefield, Lance Twitchell, Nora and Richard Dauenhauer, *Because We Cherish You* and *Háa Tuwunáagu Yís*, and myself.

73 Tlingit Language Sound Charts were created with helpful assistance from Lance Twitchell, *X̱'unei*. Any errors are mine.

Study Guide

Lance Twitchell, <u>X</u>'*unei*, M. F. A.
Assistant Professor of Native Languages
University of Alaska Southeast, Juneau, Alaska

Themes: Colonization, Language Loss, Cultural Conflict, and Language & Culture Revitalization

Colonization

Colonization in Alaska has its roots in violence, subjugation, and natural resource extraction. Studies of accounts from early Russian explorers and Alaska Native oratories show that the relationship from first contact was beneficial only to the newcomers and often resulted in death, slavery, and other forms of oppression for Alaska Natives. Tracking the history of colonization in Alaska would follow the activities of the Russian-American fur trade, various Christian missionaries, the American fur trade, boarding schools, the gold rush, fights for civil rights, the oil rush, the battle for land claims, and the aftermath of all. Today, Alaska is a complex web of social illness, evident in suicide rates, violent crime rates, declining indigenous languages, and battles between Alaska Native tribes and corporations.

Early missionaries in Alaska first tried to protect people from the violent and cruel tactics of the Russian fur trade. After America purchased Alaska from Russia, without any consideration for Alaska Native people and rights to land claims, American missionaries divided the state among ten different Christian denominations via the Comity Plan of 1890, which is sometimes referred to as the Jackson Polity for Alaska.

The boarding schools established for Native American children from the 1880s well into the 1900s were significant in the destruction of language and culture for the Tlingit. These schools forbade the use of Alaska Native languages, and often punished students violently for speaking in their ancestral tongue. In addition, throughout Alaska's history many institutions and communities have portrayed Alaska Native languages as inferior or childlike, when in actually they developed over tens of thousands of years and show relationships to people, land, and animals that show an intimate and detailed understanding of people, place, history, oratory, and spirituality.

In what modern theorists of Alaska Native and American Indian Studies are calling the neo-colonial age, many people are looking towards the acts of colonialization as causes for existing social ills, language loss, and economic difficulties among Alaska Native people. In addition, racial discrimination is still a strong factor in developing senses of self, well-being, belonging, and purpose among Alaska Native people.

Questions:
1. What are the differences between Russian and American occupancy in Alaska?
2. What similarities and differences exist between Alaska Native colonization and American Indian colonization?
3. How does treatment by colonial forces impact the world today? In what ways has life improved and in what ways has it worsened for Alaska Native people?

Resources:
- Alaska Native Epidemiology Center. *Alaska Native Health Status Report.* Alaska Native Tribal Health Consortium.
  http://www.anthc.org/chs/epicenter/upload/ANHSR.pdf
- Brown, Tricia. "Rev. Sheldon Jackson: Alaska's First General Agent of Education 1834-1909." *Lit Site Alaska.*
  http://www.litsite.org/index.cfm?section=Digital-Archives&page=Community-Life&cat=Religion&viewpost=2&ContentId=2211
- "Colonialism Wreaked Havoc on Alaska Native Peoples." *Anchorage Daily News.* 4 Feb 2009.
  http://www.adn.com/2009/02/04/679340/colonialism-wreaked-havoc-on-alaska.html
- "Ecumenism in Alaska." *Presbytery of Yukon.*
  http://www.yukonpresbytery.com/history/Issues/ecumenism.htm
- Hirshberg, Diane and Suzanne Sharp. *Thirty Years Later: The Long-Term Effect of Boarding Schools on Alaska Natives and Their Communities.* University of Alaska Anchorage: Institute of Social and Economic Research, 2005.
  http://www.iser.uaa.alaska.edu/Publications/boardingschoolfinal.pdf
- La Belle, Jim and Stacy L. Smith. *Boarding School: Historical Trauma Among Alaska's Native People.* National Resource Center for American Indian, Alaska Native, and Native Hawaiian Elders, 2005.
  http://elders.uaa.alaska.edu/reports/yr2_2boarding-school.pdf

Language Loss
Language loss affects cultural identity and Alaska Native languages are declining in fluency and use at an alarming rate. Of the twenty-one Alaska

Native languages currently studied, one (Eyak) has no native speakers of the language, and three (Northern Haida, Coast Tsimshian, Holikachuk) have fewer than ten speakers. Despite statewide efforts from universities, corporations, tribes, individuals, and other organizations, the rate of language loss is much higher than the rate of acquisition. Studies have shown that an individual generally knows five-hundred names of people or places, and when speakers are lost at a rate higher than gained, then that overall number continues to drop. This is significant because Alaska Natives have a history of place that dates back thousands of years, with the oldest known remains being over eleven thousand years old.

Questions:

1. What happens when a language goes extinct? What happens when an Alaska Native language goes extinct?
2. Who bears the responsibility of stabilizing indigenous languages and what are the major current and historical factors that result in ongoing language loss?
3. If a language is documented through recordings and teaching tools like dictionaries, what reasons exist that few speakers, if any, are currently emerging for Alaska Native languages?

Resources:

- "Alaska Native Languages: Population and Speaker Statistics." *Alaska Native Language Center*. University of Alaska Fairbanks. http://www.uaf.edu/anlc/languages/stats/
- Angayuqaq Oscar Kawagley. "How Does the Crane Keep Its Language?" *Sharing Our Pathways: A Newsletter of the Alaska Rural Systemic Initiative* 5.5 (2000). Alaska Native Knowledge Network. http://www.ankn.uaf.edu/sop/SOPv5i5.html#crane
- Fishman, Joshua. "What Do You Lose When You Lose a Language." *Stabilizing Indigenous Languages*. Northern Arizona University. http://jan.ucc.nau.edu/~jar/SIL/Fishman1.pdf
- Greymorning, Stephen. "Running the Gauntlet of an Indigenous Language Program." *Revitalizing Indigenous Languages*. Northern Arizona University. http://jan.ucc.nau.edu/~jar/RIL_2.html
- Krauss, Michael. "Status of Native American Language Endangerment." *Stabilizing Indigenous Languages*. Northern Arizona University. http://jan.ucc.nau.edu/~jar/SIL/Krauss.pdf
- Meredith, America. Racing Against Extinction: Saving Native Languages. *ahalenia.com*.
  http://www.ahalenia.com/noksi/tsalagi.html

Cultural Conflict

Alaska was not a land of equal opportunity or access. The Anti-discrimination act of 1945 was vehemently argued against by members of Alaska's Congress, who claimed that such an act would actually increase the hostility of race relations. At the time, many businesses throughout Alaska had policies about whether Alaska Native people could enter their premises, and if so where they could sit—which was often way in the back.

And even though this act passed and Alaska has made headway in many areas of race relations and cultural conflict, recent events have made national news and show that Alaska has a long ways to go in solving problems of race relations, hate crimes, and open discrimination against Alaska Native people. Many of these instances involve violence and the reduction of people to powerless and stereotyped entities, when in fact the diversity within Alaska Native people is dynamic and worth defending against senseless attacks.

In fact, a study by the Department of Justice revealed that Native Americans are three times as likely to be victims of violent crimes. Native American women are two and a half times as likely to be victims of rape or sexual assault. Of those crimes, 57% of the violent crimes and 78% of the rapes and sexual assaults will be committed by Caucasian criminals. A study by the Department of Justice found that Native Americans are the only ethnic group that receives the majority of its violent crimes from *outside* its own ethnic group.

In addition, mass media outlets, particularly radio, do nothing to assist with the rate of violent crimes and hate crimes committed against Native American people. Shock Jocks, who host radio talk shows and utilize edgy humor to hold their fame, have recently utilized racism against Alaska Native people to attract attention to their shows and to use Alaska Native people as a joke in spite of the cultural conflicts already in existence in Alaska. At the national level, radio powerhouse Rush Limbaugh has attacked Native Americans, stating that Caucasians deserve reparations after colonization for the invention of smoking cigarettes, and that Native Americans have nothing to complain about, even after losing 90 million people due to colonization, because they all have casinos.

As we move forward, we must consider the amount of education and healing that must occur in order for cultural conflict to recede and for Alaska Native issues to be discussed without hatred and pain.

Questions:

1. In moments of cultural conflict, what can be done to improve the situation at the time of the occurrence and afterwards?
2. Much of the existing racism is in existence because of power dynamics, and often seek to portray an entire collection of cultures as simple and alcoholic. What can be done to counter this collective stereotype?
3. How much have cultural relations changed over the past ten years? Twenty-five? Fifty? One hundred? What changes need to happen today?

Resources:

- D'oro, Rachel. "Shock Jocks Woody And Wilcox Suspended For Slur Against Native Alaskan Women." *Huffington Post*. 15 Apr 2008.
  http://www.huffingtonpost.com/2008/04/15/shock-jocks-woody-and-wil_n_96875.html
- Fry, Eric. "District Looks To Solve School Racism: ANB, ANS Press For Quick Action In Wake Of Recent Anti-Native Incidents." *Juneau Empire*. 29 Feb 2004.
  http://juneauempire.com/stories/022904/loc_district.shtml
- Hoklotubbe, Sara Sue. "What is a hate crime, anyway?" *Juneau Empire*. 2 Apr 2001.
  http://juneauempire.com/stories/040201/Ope_MyTurn.html
- "Jim Crow in Alaska: Articles, photographs and more documenting some of the history of racism in Alaska." *alaskool.org*.
  http://www.alaskool.org/projects/JimCrow/Jimcrow.htm
- James, Elizabeth. "The Alaska Anti-Discrimination Act – 1945." *Lit Site Alaska*.
  http://www.litsite.org/index.cfm?section=Digital-Archives&page=People-of-the-North&cat=Native-Lives-and-Traditions&viewpost=2&ContentId=3105
- Mauer, Richard. "Attack on Native draws hate-crime charges." *Anchorage Daily News*. 18 Dec. 2009.
  http://www.adn.com/2009/12/18/1061607/attack-on-native-draws-hate-crime.html#ixzz1feHFSrGY
- Limbaugh, Rush. "White Man v. Native Americans." *The Rush Limbaugh Show*. Transcript. 24 Nov. 2010.
  http://www.rushlimbaugh.com/daily/2010/11/24/white_man_v_native_americans3
- O'Malley, Julia. "When the conflict is race, don't feed the fire." *Anchorage Daily News*. 1 Sep 2010.
  http://community.adn.com/adn/node/152998#ixzz1feOhgNeT

- Perry, Steven W. Bureau of Justice Statistics. *American Indians and Crime: A BJS Statistical Profile, 1992-2002*. United States Department of Justice: Office of Tribal Justice.
  http://www.justice.gov/otj/pdf/american_indians_and_crime.pdf

Language & Culture Revitalization

Revitalizing indigenous languages is complex to say the least. The vast majority of Alaska Native language speakers are over seventy years old, and Alaska Natives have the shortest life expectancy out of any ethnic group in Alaska. That means that these languages are living on borrowed time. There are social factors involved, webs of them, as Alaska Native languages were violently removed from their populations and replaced with a language full of hateful ideals and terminology towards Alaska Native people.

In addition, there are at times hard feelings towards older generations for letting the language go, but we must understand that everything was at stake and languages were often sacrificed in order to protect land and subsistence rights. In addition, children were and often still are humiliated and imitated for having a thick village accent. But now we find ourselves in a time when the death of Alaska Native languages is right around the corner as more and more speakers pass away and fewer and fewer commit the time and resources necessary to learn a dying language.

Still, committed groups work diligently in classrooms and immersion camps to keep languages going. At one time, there was shame involved in speaking these languages, but now they are being used in grocery stores and other public places. Those who work to revitalize Alaska Native languages feel a unity among one another and an incredible sense of urgency as many call for the last possible push to keep these languages alive and revived in everyday use.

The most important place for this fight is in the home. Once the language is in the home, then it is in a safe place. As students and teachers of language, many people throughout Alaska are hoping for a time when children are speaking from birth and enriching themselves with their ancestral language and a version of English that does not belittle or insult Alaska Native people or their ancestors.

In order for languages to succeed in the coming years, communities, universities, and other organizations will have to unite their efforts in order to maximize the amount of effort and the impact of activities around language revitalization. The next twenty years will have to see an unprecedented sense of unity in order to keep Alaska Native languages from continuing to die off in the aftermath of colonialization and the violence that comes with it.

Questions:
1. What are some things that you can do right now to help Alaska Native language revitalization?
2. What kinds of things must change in your community in order to help facilitate Alaska Native language revitalization?
3. What are the benefits of knowing more than one language? What are the benefits of knowing the ancestral language of a place in which you live?

Resources:
- Anonby, Stan J. "Reversing Language Shift: Can Kwak'wala Be Revived." *Revitalizing Indigenous Languages*. Northern Arizona University. http://jan.ucc.nau.edu/~jar/RIL_4.html
- Argetsinger, Tim. "Alaska Native Language Resources." *Alaskool.org*. Jan 2008.
  http://www.alaskool.org/language/LanguageRevitalization.htm
- Cantoni, Gina P. "Using TPR-Storytelling to Develop Fluency and Literacy in Native American Languages." *Revitalizing Indigenous Languages*. Northern Arizona University.
  http://jan.ucc.nau.edu/~jar/RIL_5.html
- Edwards, Keri. "575+ Tlingit Verbs." *Goldbelt Heritage Foundation*. http://www.goldbeltheritage.org/verbs/verbs/tlingit/1
- "Language Resources." *Sealaska Heritage Institute*.
  http://www.sealaskaheritage.org/programs/language_resources.htm
- Littlebear, Richard. "Some Rare and Radical Ideas for Keeping Indigenous Languages Alive." *Revitalizing Indigenous Languages*. Northern Arizona University.
  http://jan.ucc.nau.edu/~jar/RIL_1.html#poem
- "Repatriated Bones, Unrepatriated Spirits." *Revitalizing Indigenous Languages*. Northern Arizona University.
  http://jan.ucc.nau.edu/~jar/RIL_1.html#poem
- Reyhner, Jon. "Some Basics of Indigenous Language Revitalization." *Revitalizing Indigenous Languages*. Northern Arizona University.
  http://jan.ucc.nau.edu/~jar/RIL_Intro.html
- "Tlingit Language Teaching And Learning Aids." *Alaskool.com*.
  http://www.alaskool.org/language/indexing/tlingindex.htm
- Twitchell, Lance X̱'unei. "Tlingit Pronouns and Possessive Pronouns." *Youtube*.   http://www.youtube.com/watch?v=3UaIMcGwjro

Overall Study Questions and Writing Topics

1. Are there many different points of view in the poems?
2. How does the point of view affect the poem?
3. What is the mood of the collection?
4. How does the collection as a whole tell a story? What story does it tell?
5. How does the history of language loss affect new generations of Tlingit?
6. What role does multiculturalism play in colonization, language loss, cultural conflict, and language & culture revitalization?
7. When thinking about the subject matter in this collection of poems, what will Alaska look like in fifty years? How will the voices in the poem sound at that time?

About the Author

Vivian Faith Prescott was born and raised in Wrangell, Alaska and lives in Sitka, Alaska. She has a Ph.D. in Cross Cultural Studies and an MFA from the University of Alaska, Anchorage. Vivian is Co-Director of Raven's Blanket, a non-profit designed to perpetuate the cultural wellness and traditions of Indigenous peoples and promote artistic works by Alaskans. She is of Sáami, Suomalainen, and Irish descent (among others) and her children are Tlingit of the T'akdéintaan clan/Snail House. She is adopted into the T'akdéintaan clan and her Tlingit name is *Yéilk' Tlaa*, Mother of Cute Little Raven. Vivian also co-facilitates writers' groups for teenagers and adults. Vivian is a Pushcart Prize and Best of the Net nominee and a recipient of the Jason Wenger Award for Literary Excellence. She was a finalist for the 2008 and 2009 Joy Harjo Award from *Cutthroat: a Journal of the Arts* and was awarded Honorable Mention in *Boulevard's* Poetry Contest for Emerging Writers (2009). She also received honorable mention in the Harold McCracken poetry contest and was a finalist in the Winning Writers War Poetry contest. In addition to her poetry awards, Vivian received the Cortland Auser award from the American Association of Ethnic Studies.

Website: http://www.vivianfaithprescott.com

Blog: http://planetalaska.blogspot.com

Vivian Faith Prescott
111 A Polaris Ave
Kodiak, Alaska 99615
doctorviv@hotmail.com

www.ingramcontent.com/pod-product-compliance
Lightning Source LLC
Chambersburg PA
CBHW071237020426
42333CB00015B/1511